# TURN YOUR RADIO ON

## GOSPEL SONGS FROM THE GOOD OLD DAYS

Created and Arranged by Marty Parks

lillenas
PUBLISHING COMPANY
lillenas.com

# Contents

# Turn Your Radio On

Words and Music by
ALBERT E. BRUMLEY
*Arr. by Marty Parks*

With a bounce! ♩ = ca. 134 (♫ = ♩♪ triplet)

LADIES div.
mf
8
Turn your ra - di - o on,
Turn your ra - di - o on,
Turn your ra - di - o
E♭
E♭
10
on, turn your ra - di - o on!
turn your ra - di - o on!
turn your ra - di - o on!
If you
Get a lit - tle
E♭
B♭
F7
B♭7
13
wan - na hear the songs of Zi - on com - in' from the land of end - less
taste of joy a - wait - ing, get a lit - tle heav - en in your
E♭6
E♭6
E♭7/G
A♭7
A♭7/C

CD: 2 1st time
CD: 4 2nd time
16
Get in touch with God,
spring; Get in touch with God, turn your ra - di - o
soul; Get in touch with God, turn your ra - di - o
E♭ N.C. E♭ N.C. E♭/B♭ B♭7
19
cresc.
f
turn your ra - di - o on!
on! Turn your ra - di - o on,
on!
cresc.
f
E♭7 A♭ E♭ N.C. E♭ E♭2
f
22
and lis - ten to the mu - sic in the air; Turn your ra - di - o
E♭ E♭7/G A♭7 A♭7/C E♭ N.C.

25
on, heav-en's glo - ry share.
E♭ E♭7/B♭ A♭/B♭ E♭ A♭/E♭ E♭ B♭ F7/C
28
Turn the lights down low, and list-ten to the
B♭7/D B♭ E♭ E♭2 E♭ E♭7/G
31
Get in touch with God;
Mas - ter's ra - di - o,
Get in touch with
A♭7 A♭7/C E♭ N.C. E♭ N.C.

34
CD: 5 2nd time
1
CD: 3
Turn your ra - di - o
on!
God;
1
E♭/B♭
B♭7
E♭7
A♭7
E♭
N.C.
E♭
C7
38
(to pg. 4, meas. 5)
2. Bro - ther, lis - ten
MEN unis. mf
F7
B♭7
A♭7
B♭9
(to pg. 4, meas. 5)
41
2
Get in touch with God;
on!
Get in touch with
2
E♭
E♭7
E♭7/B♭
A♭
N.C.
E♭

44
Turn your ra - di - o on!
Get in
Get in touch with
God;
E♭/B♭
B♭7
E♭
A♭/E♭
A♭/B♭
E♭
N.C.
47
Get in touch with God;
Turn your ra - di - o
touch, touch with God;
God, with God;
Turn your ra - di - o
Fm
F♯°/A
E♭/B♭
N.C.
B♭
A♭/B♭
F♯°/B♭
50
on!
on! Turn your ra - di - o on!
E♭
E♭7/B♭
A♭
A♭m/F
E♭
E♭/B♭
E♭
8vb

# God Shall Wipe Away All Tears

J. R. BAXTER, JR. and
WESLEY H. DANIEL
*Arr. by Marty Parks*

Reflectively ♩ = ca. 68

11
tears; When we join the
tears; No more part - ings
C7sus C7 F
14
saints and wear a robe and crown,
come to mar that hap - py song,
F F7/A B♭ F
CD: 7 1st time
CD: 10 2nd time
17
God shall wipe a - way all tears.
God shall wipe a - way all tears.
F F/C F°/D C7 F Gm/F

20
God shall wipe a - way all the
F7 Gm/F F7 B♭ B♭ B♭m6
23
tears from ev - 'ry eye; Give us joy for all our
F G♯°/F F F F F Am7/E G9/D
27
fears; When we meet Him
Gm7 C7 C7♯5 F

30
2nd time to Coda
(to pg. 15, meas. 53)
in that home be - yond the sky,
F
F7/A
B♭
F
2nd time to Coda
(to pg. 15, meas. 53)
33
CD: 8
God shall wipe a - way all tears.
F
F/C
F°/D
C7
F
Dm7
G6
G7
G7♯5
37
DUET (or 2-part Choir)
mp
2. When the pearl - y gates un - fold for you and me,
mp
C
C7/E
F6
F
C

41
God shall wipe a - way all tears;
C
C
D 9/A
G 7sus
G 7
45
When we see the Christ who set the cap-tive free,
C
C 7/E
F 6
F
C
49
CD: 9
D.S. al Coda
(to pg. 10, meas. 5)
God shall wipe a - way all tears.
D.S. al Coda
(to pg. 10, meas. 5)
C
C/G
C°/A
G 7
C
B♭/C
C 7♯5

CODA
God shall wipe a - way all tears, all
CODA
tears. God shall wipe a - way all
tears.
rit.

# Dwelling in Beulah Land

Words and Music by
C. AUSTIN MILES
*Arr. by Marty Parks*

With assurance and joy! ♩ = ca. 128 (♫ = ♩ ♪ triplet)

11
set on ev - 'ry hand. Doubt and fear and
see the way He planned. Dwell - ing in the
C C9 F7 F6 Cm/F F7 B♭ Cm/B♭ B♭ E♭/B♭
14
things of earth in vain to me are call - ing;
Spir - it here, I learn of full sal - va - tion;
B♭ E♭/B♭ B♭ B♭/F F6 F7 B♭
CD: 12 1st time
CD: 14 2nd time
17
None of these shall move me from Beu - lah
Glad - ly will I tar - ry in Beu - lah
E♭ F/E♭ E♭ B♭/F B♭/D E♭ B♭/F Cm/F F7

CHOIR both times
Land.
Land. I'm liv - ing on the moun - tain, un - der - neath a cloud - less
B♭ F sus B♭ E♭/B♭ B♭ B♭4/2 B♭ B°7
sky; I'm drink - ing at the foun - tain that nev - er shall run
sky; Praise God,
F7/C F7 F7 E♭/F F B♭ B♭/F B♭/D C7 C6 C C9
dry. O yes, I'm feast - ing on the man - na from a boun - ti - ful sup -
F7 F C7/G F7/A B♭ B♭4/2 B♭ B♭ B♭/D E♭6 E♭

32
CD: 15 2nd time
ply; For I am dwell - ing in Beu - lah
B♭/D N.C. B♭/F B♭/D E♭ B♭/F Cm/F F7
8vb
35
1
CD: 13
(to pg. 16, meas. 5)
Land!
1
(to pg. 16, meas. 5)
B♭ E♭/B♭ E♭/F B♭ B♭/F B♭/D E♭ F6 Cm/F F7
39
2
Cued notes opt.
mp
Land!
I'm liv - ing
I'm liv - ing on the
mp
2
B♭ E♭/B♭ B♭ Cm7/F B♭ B♭/F E♭/F
mp

42
on the moun - tain, un - der - neath a cloud - less sky;
moun - tain, un - der - neath a cloud - less sky; I'm
B♭ B♭/F B♭2 B°7 F/C F
3 3
45
I'm drink - ing at the foun - tain, nev - er shall run
drink - ing at the foun - tain that nev - er shall run
F7/C F7 E♭/F B♭ B♭/F C7 C7/G C9/G
48
f
dry. O yes, I'm feast - ing on the man - na from a
dry.
F7 C7/G F7/A B♭ B♭4/2 B♭ B♭ B♭/D

51
bountiful supply; For I am dwelling in Beulah
E♭6 E♭ B♭/D N.C. B♭/F B♭/D E♭ B♭/F Cm/F F7
55
Land, Beulah Land! Dwelling in Beulah
Gm Gm/F E♭ B♭/F B♭/D E♭ B♭/F F9
59
Land!
Land, in Beulah Land!
B♭ B♭ B♭ N.C.

# Over the Sunset Mountains

Words and Music by
JOHN W. PETERSON
*Arr. by Marty Parks*

13
In the arms of Je - sus,
In - to the arms of Je - sus,
mel.
F
F/E♭
D7
G7
G7
17
CD: 17
He who loved me so.
He who has loved me so.
C7/E
C7
C7/G
C9
C6
C7
F
F6
Cm/F
F7
21
CHOIR parts (both times)
mf
O - ver the sun - set moun -
B♭
Gm7
C9
F2
F
FM7

24
2nd time to Coda
(to pg. 26, meas. 55)
tains heav - en a - waits for me.
2nd time to Coda
(to pg. 26, meas. 55)
Dm2 Dm Dm7 Gm Gm2 Gm C7 C9 F2 F
28
Oh, o - ver the sun - set
F Eb/G F7/A Bb Gm7 C9
31
moun - tains Je - sus, my Sav - ior, I'll
Am Am7 D7 Gm Gm2 Gm C7

35
CD: 18
see.
Oo.
F2 F Dm2 Dm F/G Gm Dm/C C♭9 7
39
SOLO expressively
mp
Toil - ing will all be end - ed,
F F/E♭ D7 G7 G7
mp
43
shad - ows will flee a - way;
C7/E C7 C7/G C13 B♭2/D C9/E F2 F FM7 C13

47
Sor-row will be for - got - ten,
F
F/E♭
D7
G7
G7
51
CD: 19
D.S. al Coda
(to pg. 23, meas. 21)
Oh, what a won - der - ful day!
C7/E
C7
C7/G
C9
C6
C7
F
F6
Cm/F
F7
55
CODA
Oh, o - ver the sun - set
E♭/G
F7
B♭
Gm7

58
moun - tains
Je - sus, my Sav - ior, I'll
Am Am7 D2 D Gm Gm2 Gm C7 C9
62
see.
mp
Je - sus, my Sav - ior,
F Am7/E Dm7 B♭m6 Gm Gm2 Gm C7
66
rit.
I'll see.
C9 C6 C♭9/7 F F2 F F2
p

# My God Is Real

Words and Music by
KENNETH MORRIS
*Arr. by Marty Parks*

5
There are some things I may not
mf
There are some things
G D6 D7 G G7/B
7
know, There are some plac - es I can't
I may not know; Plac - es I can't
C C#°7 G/D D7
9
go; But I am sure of this one
go, can't go. But I am sure
G G6 G D6 D7 G G7/B

CD: 22
11
thing, That God is real for I can feel Him deep with-
of this one thing: Real, for I can feel Him deep with-
C C♯°7 G/D D7 C/D D7
13
in. My God is real, real in my
in, deep with-in. My God is real,
G C/G G G7 G7♯5 C C7
15
soul; My God is real for He has washed and made me
real in my soul; Real, for He has washed and made me
G C/G G G F♯ G/F E7 A7

17
whole. His love for me is like pure
whole, made me whole. His love for me
D A7/E D7 G G7/B
CD: 25 2nd time
2nd time to Coda
(to pg. 33, meas. 32)
19
gold; My God is real for I can feel Him in my
is like pure gold; Real, feel
C C♯°7 G/D D7
2nd time to Coda
(to pg. 33, meas. 32)
8vb
CD: 23
21
soul!
Him in my soul.
G C7/G G C♯°7 G/D D7 C/D D7
8vb

23
mp
I can - not tell just how you
G
C 7/G
G
D 6
D 7
G
G 9/B
G 7/B
mp
25
felt when Je - sus took your sins a -
C
C♯°7
G/D
D 7
27
mf
way.
Oo,
But since that day,
Yes, since that
mf
G
D 6
D 7
G
G 7/B
cresc.
mf

CD: 24
29
Oo, Ah! Real, feel
hour; God has been real, for I can feel His ho - ly
C C#°7 G/D D7
D.S. al Coda CODA
(to pg. 30, meas. 14)
31
My God is soul! My God is
f
His ho - ly pow'r! Him in my soul!
pow'r!
D.S. al Coda CODA
(to pg. 30, meas. 14)
G C/G G G7 G7♯5 G C7/G G C#°7

33
real for I can feel Him in my soul!
sub. p
Real, feel Him in my soul! My God is
sub. p
G/D D7 G C7/G G G/B
8vb
8vb
35
real; My God is real!
mp
My God is
mp
C7 C9 G G/B
p
37
real; My God is real!
mf
My God is
mf
C7 C9 G/D Am G Am/G G7/D
mp

39
real;
My God is
real!
My God is
f
C7
C9
G
Am/D
G
Am/G
G7/D
mf
41
real;
My God is
C7
C9
C7
C9
f
8vb
43
real!
G
Am/D
G
Am/G
G
N.C.
G

# How Long Has It Been?

Words and Music by
MOSIE LISTER
*Arr. by Marty Parks*

Reflectively ♩ = ca. 72

11
told Him your heart's hid - den se - crets?
prayed to the Lord up in heav - en?
D♭ D♭° E♭/D♭ D♭ E♭/D♭ D♭ D♭/A♭ A♭
CHOIR parts (both times)
mf
14
How long since you
How long since you
mf
A♭2 Fm E♭7 F♯°7/E♭
mf
16
prayed? How long since you
knew that He'd an - swer
E♭7 C7 Fm C7/E

18
stayed on your knees 'til the light shone
you, and would keep you the long night
Fm Fm7 B♭9 B♭7 B♭13
CD: 27 1st time
CD: 29 2nd time
1st time: MEN melody, LADIES no cues
2nd time: LADIES only (2-part)
21
dim.
mp
through? How
through? How
E♭ B♭7sus/F B♭7/F E♭/G E♭7
23
long has it been since your mind felt at
long has it been since you woke with the
A♭ A♭° D♭/A♭ A♭ A♭4/2 A♭ A♭° D♭/A♭
mp

26
ease? How long since your heart knew no
dawn, and felt that the day's worth the
A♭ C7 D♭ D♭° E♭/D♭ D♭ E♭/D♭ D♭
29
CHOIR parts (both times)
mf
bur - den? Can you call Him your
liv - ing?
mf
Can you call Him your
D♭/A♭ A♭ A♭ D♭2 D♭ D♭7
mf
32
Friend? How long has it been since you
Friend? How long has it been
C7 Fm2 Fm Fm7 B♭ B♭7/F

35
1
knew that He cared for you?
A♭/E♭
A♭6/E♭
E♭6
E♭7
D♭2
D♭
38
CD: 28
(to pg. 36, meas. 7)
mp
2. How
A♭2/C
A♭/C
B♭m2
B♭m
dim.
E♭13
E♭7
41
2
CD: 30
f
you?
Can you call Him your
A♭
A♭/E♭
A♭/C
D♭2
D♭

44
Friend? How long has it been since you
C sus C Fm2 Fm B♭ B♭7
47
dim.
knew that He cared for you?
dim.
A♭/E♭ A♭6/E♭ E♭6 E♭7 A♭
dim.
50
rit.
mp
For you?
mp
D♭/A♭ A♭ A♭ A♭
rit.
mp

# God's Choir

Words and Music by
RAY OVERHOLT
*Arr. by Marty Parks*

CD: 32
rit.
Bright and rhythmic ♩ = ca. 94
1st time: CHOIR parts
2nd time: CHOIR unison
mf
writ-ten for a choir way up there.
1. I heard the
(2. I fell down)
mf
Bright and rhythmic ♩ = ca. 94
C2/G G7 C F/G C G6 G9 B7
rit.
mf
an - gels sing: "Glo - ry, hal - le - lu - jah!" a
on my knees when that cho - rus end - ed, they
C C7 F C
might - y cho - rus way up high; I heard the
shout - ed out a glad "A - men." I fell down
C Gsus G G6 G9 B7

CD: 33 1st time
CD: 35 2nd time
15
an - gels sing: "Praise the name of Je - sus!"
on my knees, prayed, that when in heav - en,
C C7 F C
CHOIR parts (both times)
17
sing - ing in God's choir in the sky.
I would hear that choir once a - gain.
I heard a
f
G7/D G7 F/G G7 C F/G C Dm7 C7/E
19
thou - sand trum - pets sound - ing out His glo - ry;
F F C
f

21
Tell - ing the sto - ry how He came to earth to die. I heard a
G7/D G7 C Dm7 C7/E
23
mil - lion voic - es praise the name of Je - sus;
F F C
25
1 CD: 34
Sing - ing in God's choir in the sky.
G7/D F/G G7 F/G G7 1 C F/C C°/G C

27
(to pg. 43, meas. 11)
2
mf
2. I fell down sky.
G7 F/G G7 C G6 G9 B7
C F/C C°/G C G/B
30
CD: 36
f
I heard a
Em/A A6 Em/A D6/A A D Dsus/E D7/F♯
34
thou - sand trum - pets sound - ing out His glo - ry;
thou - sand trum - pets, thou - sand trum - pets
G G D

36
Tell - ing the sto - ry how He came to earth to die. I heard a
A7/E A7 D G/E D7/F♯
38
mil - lion voic - es praise the name of Je - sus;
mil - lion voic - es, mil - lion voic - es
G G D
40
CD: 37 2nd time
1 (to pg. 46, meas. 34)
2
Sing - ing in God's choir in the sky. I heard a sky.
A7/E A7 G/A A7 D G/A D G/E D7/F♯ D G/A D

43
Sing - ing in God's choir in the sky.
A7/E G/A A7 G/A A7 D G/A D
45
ff
Sing - ing in God's choir in the sky.
A7/E A7 N.C. Em/A C♯/A D
48
D D Em/A C♯/A D
8vb

# Calvary Covers It All

Words and Music by
ETHEL ROBINSON TAYLOR
*Arr. by Marty Parks*

11
mes - sage that came to my heart;
Je - sus, my cru - ci - fied Lord;
Gm Cm Fm
14
2nd time: MEN unison
mp
How that Je - sus a - lone for my
My re - demp - tion com - plete I then
B♭9sus B♭9 E♭2 E♭ E♭M7 D♭6/E♭
17
CHOIR parts (both times)
mp
sin did a - tone,
found at His feet,
And Cal - va - ry
mp
A♭2 A♭ A♭M7 A♭m/F E♭2/B♭ E♭/B♭

CD: 39 1st time
CD: 41 2nd time
20
cov - ers it all.
B♭ A♭/B♭ F°/B♭ E♭ A♭m/F
23
mf
Cal - va - ry cov - ers it all,
E♭ A♭6 A♭ Gm
26
my past, with its sin and
A♭2 A♭ B♭7 Cm Fm B♭7

29
stain; My guilt and de -
E♭2 E♭ E♭M7 E♭7 A♭2 A♭
32
spair Je - sus took on Him there, And
A♭ A♭6 A♭7 E♭ Cm7 A♭m/C♭
35
Cal - va - ry cov - ers it all.
E♭2/B♭ E♭/B♭ B♭ A♭/B♭ F°/B♭
1
E♭

38
CD: 40
(to pg. 49, meas. 7)
LADIES unis. mp
2. How
A♭m/F
E♭
A♭m/F
(to pg. 49, meas. 7)
41
2
CD: 42
all.
f
Cal - va - ry
f
2
E♭
E♭/D♭
B
E
f
44
cov - ers it all,
my
A 6
A
G♯m
A 2
A
B 7

47
past, with its sin and stain;
C♯m F♯m B7 E2 E EM7
50
My guilt and de - spair Je - sus
E7 A2 A A A6 A7
53
took on Him there, And Cal - va - ry
E C♯m Am/C E2/B E/B

56
cov - ers it all.
B
A/B
F♯°/B
E
F♯°
59
mf
dim.
mp
Cal - va - ry cov - ers it
E2/B
E/B
B
A/B
A/B
Am6/B
62
rit.
all.
E
D/E
Am6/E
E2
mp rit.

# When God Dips His Love in My Heart

Words and Music by
CLEAVANT DERRICKS
*Arr. by Marty Parks*

10
pen of love in my heart, And
step up Cal - v'ry's rug - ged way, To
F
Cm/A
B♭
E♭/B♭
B♭
F
Gm/F
F
13
writes my soul a mes - sage He wants me to
give His life com - plete - ly and bring a bet - ter
F
Gm/C
Dm7
G
G9
16
know; His Spir - it, all di - vine, fills this
way; My life was steeped in sin, but in
C9
F
Gm/C
F
Cm/A

CD: 44 1st time
CHOIR parts (both times)
CD: 46 2nd time
19
sin - ful soul of mine, When God dips His
love He took me in; His blood washed a -
B♭ E♭/B♭ B♭ F Dm B♭m6/D♭
22
love in my heart.
way ev - 'ry stain.
f
Well, I said I would - n't
F/C C9 N.C. F
25
tell it to a liv - ing soul, How He brought sal -
F6 B♭/F F Cm/A

27
va - tion and He made me whole, But I found I could - n't
B♭
F
29
hide such love as Je - sus did im - part.
F
D m
G 9
C 7
B♭m6/D♭
32
Laugh and it makes me
Well, it makes me laugh and it makes me
C 7
F
G m/C

34
cry, sets my sin - ful soul on fire; When
cry and it sets my sin - ful soul on fire, on fire;
F Cm/A B♭6 B♭ F C/E
37
1 CD: 45
God dips His love in my heart.
Dm B♭m6/D♭ F/C C9 F F/C F6
41
(to pg. 56, meas. 9)
TRIO mf
2 CD: 47
2. He heart,
mf
C6 A♭m/C Gm N.C. (to pg. 56, meas. 9) F F/C
mf

44
in my heart!
Well, I said I would-n't
Well, I said I would-n't
F
Cm6/E♭
D sus
D6
8vb
47
tell it,
How He brought sal-
tell it to a liv-ing soul, How He brought sal-
G
G
Dm/B
49
va-tion,
I can't
va-tion and He made me whole, But I found I could-n't
C
G
C/D
8vb

51
hide such love, O as Je - sus did im -
hide such love as Je - sus did im - part.
G
G/B
A 9
D
A
54
part.
Laugh and it makes me
Well, it makes me laugh and it makes me
D 7
G
Am/D
8vb
56
cry, sets my sin - ful soul on fire; When
cry and it sets my sin - ful soul on fire, on fire;
G
Dm/B
C
G
D/F♯
8vb

59
God dips His love in my heart, in my heart! When
Em
Cm6/E♭
G/D
D9
Em
Em7
A9
8vb
63
God dips His love in my heart, in my
G/D
Dsus
D6
D9
G
C/G
8vb
67
heart!
heart! Way down in - a my heart!
G
G
G
D6
G

# I Know Who Holds Tomorrow

Words and Music by
IRA STANPHILL
*Arr. by Marty Parks*

CHOIR parts (both times)
5
live from day to day; I don't
bring me pov - er - ty; But the
E♭/B♭ F/B♭ E♭/B♭ B♭ B♭9
mf
7
bor - row from its sun - shine, for its
One who feeds the spar - row is the
E♭ F/E♭ E♭ B♭ G6 G7
MEN unison (2nd time)
mp
9
skies may turn to gray.
One Who stands by me.
I don't
for its skies may turn to gray.
And the
is the One Who stands by me.
mp
C C6 C7 C6 C7 Fsus F E♭/F F
(♭)
mp

11
wor - ry o'er the fu - ture, for I
path that is my por - tion may be
B♭
B♭
B♭2
CHOIR parts (both times)
13
mf
know what Je - sus said; And to -
through the flame or flood; But His
mf
E♭
F/E♭
E♭
B♭
B♭9
mf
15
day I'll walk be - side Him, for He
pres - ence goes be - fore me, and I'm
E♭
F/E♭
E♭
B♭
E♭/G
E♭m6/G♭

CD: 49 1st time
CD: 51 2nd time
17
knows what lies a - head.
cov - ered with His blood.
Man - y
f
B♭/F F6 F9 F6 F B♭ B♭9
19
f
Man - y things a - bout to - mor - row
things a - bout to - mor - row I don't
E♭ E♭/B♭ B♭ B♭/A
f
21
I don't seem to un - der - stand;
seem to un - der - stand;
But I
Gm Gm7 C9 F7sus F7 E♭/F F

23
know Who holds to - mor - row, and I
B♭
B♭9
E♭
E♭/G
E♭m6/G♭
25
know Who holds my hand.
B♭/F
F6
F
F7
1
B♭
E♭
28
CD: 50
(to pg. 64, meas. 3)
mp
2
CD: 52
2. I don't
hand.
E♭m
E♭sus
E♭m
E♭/F
mf
B♭
B♭/A

31
rit.
a tempo
Yes, I know Who holds to -
F/G FM7/G F6/G F/G G7 C C9
rit.
a tempo
33
mor - row, and I know He holds my
F F/A Fm6/A♭ C/G N.C. Dm/G G6 G7
36
rit.
ff
(8)
hand! He holds my hand!
ff
F F/A Fm6 Fm C
(8)
ff rit.
8vb

# I'm Feeling Fine

Words and Music by
MOSIE LISTER
*Arr. by Marty Parks*

*1st time:* CHOIR *parts*
*2nd time:* SOLO *(Choir opt. "Oohs")*

**CD: 53** Brightly! ♩ = ca. 104

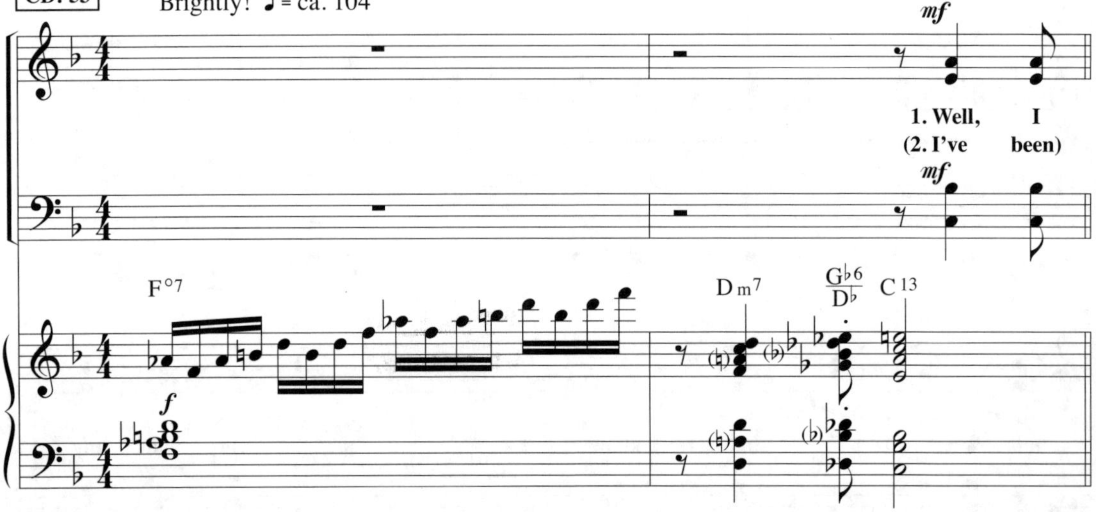


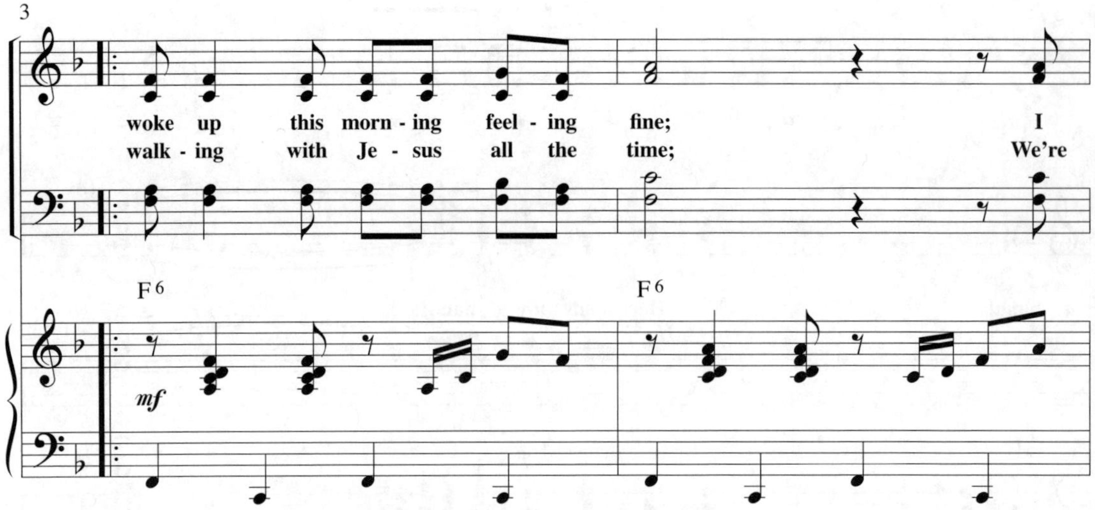

5
woke up with heav - en on my mind. I
walk - ing and talk - ing as we climb. We're
C7 D♭7 C7 F6 F6/A
7
woke up with joy in my soul, 'Cause I
trav - 'ling a road to the sky, Where I
B♭ B♭m F6
9
knew the Lord had con - trol. Well, I
know I'll live when I die. He's been
G G7 Dm/C C C13

11
knew I was walk - in' in the light, 'Cause I'd
tell - ing me all a - bout that land, And He
F6
F6
13
been on my knees in the night. And I'd
tells me that ev - 'ry - thing is grand; And He
C7
D♭7
C7
F6
F6/A
CD: 54 1st time
CD: 56 2nd time
15
prayed till the Lord gave a sign; And
says that a home will be mine; And
B♭
B♭m
F6

CHOIR (both times)
17
Well, I'm
f
now I'm feel - ing might - y fine!
now I'm feel - ing might - y fine!
C
D♯°
G
C
F 6
B♭
C
F 6
feel - ing, feel - ing might - y fine, I've got
19
f
Feel - ing might - y fine, feel - ing might - y fine;
f
F 6
C 9
G
f
heav - en on my mind; Don't you
21
Heav - en on my mind, heav - en on my mind.
C 9
F 6

23
know I want to go Where the
O I want to go, yes, I want to go;
B♭7
F6
25
milk and hon - ey flow! There's a
Go to where the milk and hon - ey flow.
G7
C9
27
light that al - ways shines Down in -
Light that al - ways shines, light that al - ways shines;
F6
C9/G

29
side this heart of mine; I've got
In this heart of mine, in this heart of mine.
C9
F6
31
heav - en, heav - en on my mind, And I'm
Heav - en on my mind, heav - en on my mind;
B♭
B♭7
F6
CD: 55 1st time
CD: 57 2nd time
33
feel - ing, feel - ing might - y fine!
Now I'm feel - ing, feel - ing might - y fine.
C7
F
B♭
F

35
1
SOLO (Choir opt. "Oohs")
mf
(to pg. 70, meas. 3)
2. I've been
1 F°7
D m7
G♭6 / D♭
C 13
(to pg. 70, meas. 3)
37
2
Well, I'm
2
F 6
C m / F
B♭ / F
F 7
D 7
C / D
D 9
8vb
39
feel - ing, feel - ing might - y fine, I've got
Feel - ing might - y fine, feel - ing might - y fine;
Feel - ing might - y, feel - ing might - y fine;
G 6
D 7 / A

41
heav - en on my mind; Don't you
Heav - en on my mind, heav - en on my mind.
I've got heav - en, heav - en on my mind.
D7 D9 G6
43
know I want to go Where the
O I want to go, yes, I want to go;
O I want to, yes, I want to go;
C9 G6
8vb
45
milk and hon - ey flow! There's a
Go to where the milk and hon - ey flow.
Go to where the milk and hon - ey flow.
A7 D7
8vb 8vb 8vb

light that al - ways shines Down in -
47
Light that al - ways shines, light that al - ways shines;
There's a light that, light that al - ways shines;
G 6
D 7
A
side this heart of mine; I've got
49
In this heart of mine, in this heart of mine.
Down in - side, in side this heart of mine.
D 7
D 9
G 6
heav - en, heav - en on my mind, And I'm
51
Heav - en on my mind, heav - en on my mind;
I've got heav - en, heav - en on my mind;
C 9
C 9
E
G 6
8vb

53
feel - ing, feel - ing might - y fine! I've got
Now I'm feel - ing, feel - ing might - y fine.
D7 G C G
8vb
55
heav - en,
Heav - en, heav - en on my mind; And
C9 C9/E G6
57
now I'm feel - ing fine!
G G°7 Am7 Cm6/G G6 G

# When We See Christ

Words and Music by
ESTHER KERR RUSTHOI
*Arr. by Marty Parks*

10
when we see Christ. One glimpse of
A♭ A♭+ D♭ D♭/A♭ D♭ D♭9 D♭7/F
13
His dear face all sor - row will e - rase;
G♭ E♭m A♭ A♭9 G♭/D♭ D♭
8vb
2nd time to Coda
(to pg. 84, meas. 40)
CD: 61 2nd time
16
So brave - ly run the race 'til we see
2nd time to Coda
(to pg. 84, meas. 40)
D♭ D♭° D♭ E♭m A♭7 A♭ A♭7 G♭/A♭ A♭7
8vb

CD: 59
19
Christ.
D♭
G♭m/E♭
D♭2/F
D♭/F
22
mp
Oft - times the day seems long, our
mp
E♭m7/A♭
G♭/A♭
D♭2
D♭
E♭m/D♭
E°/D♭
D♭
mp
25
tri - als hard to bear; We're tempt - ed to com -
mel.
G♭
G♭m/E♭
A♭♭9 7
D♭2
D♭
D♭/F
A♭
F°/A

28
mf
plain, to murmer and de - spair. But
A♭9 G♭/D♭ D♭ D♭° D♭ G♭/A♭
31
mel.
Christ will soon ap - pear to catch His Bride a -
D♭2 D♭ E♭m/D♭ E°/D♭ D♭ G♭ A♭/G♭ G♭
34
mel.
way; All tears for - ev - er o - ver in
D♭/F D♭ D♭/F G♭ E♭m7 Fm B♭m B♭m/A♭

CD: 60
D.S. al Coda
(to pg. 80, meas. 5)
37
God's e - ter - nal day. It will be
D.S. al Coda
(to pg. 80, meas. 5)
E♭m/G♭ E♭m D♭/A♭ A♭7 D♭ D♭ D♭/F A♭7/E♭ D♭9/F
40
CODA
Christ. One glimpse of His dear face all sor - row
CODA
D♭ D♭ D♭9 D♭7/F G♭ E♭m7 A♭ A♭9
44
will e - rase; So brave - ly run the race
G♭/D♭ D♭ D♭ D♭° D♭ E♭m7 A♭7
8vb
8vb

47
'til we see Christ.
So brave - ly
A♭ A♭7 G♭/A♭ A♭7 D♭ D♭ D♭° D♭
8vb
50
run the race
'til we see Christ.
E♭m7 A♭7 A♭ A♭7 G♭/A♭ A♭7 A
53
ff
'Til we see Christ!
F♯m7 B/F♯ F♯m7 D♭ D♭ N.C.
8vb